In a day when there is a quick fix mindset, an *abracadabra* expectation and an *open sesame* orientation placed on the spiritual discipline of prayer, Dr. Fletcher Law subjects prayer to its related conditions in Scripture. He straightens out the interrogative concerns revolving around prayer and transforms them into exclamatory responses that find their place in Scripture. This book is simple and yet has the potential to have a stupendous impact on those who are willing to pray according to the Word of God, believing that prayer is not overcoming God's reluctance; rather, it is laying hold to God's willingness. This book is for those who desire to go beyond the gates of thanksgiving in order to enter into the courts of praise through praying according to Scripture.

Dr. Robert Smith, Jr.
Beeson Divinity School, Charles T. Carter Baptist Chair, Samford University

It is my honor to recommend the book *How Prayer Really Works: According to Scripture* by the Reverend Doctor Fletcher Law. In this concise book the author answers probing questions concerning the mystery and importance of prayer. I would suggest each reader has their Bible in hand as they peruse each page. What greater source for knowing more about this great mystery (prayer) than the Holy Scriptures? The author has done much Scriptural research in compiling this book. If you take advantage of his research, this book will become alive. The Disciples of Jesus asked Jesus to teach them how to pray and Dr. Law deals with this, as well as many other aspects of prayer. You will want to study and listen to the Spirit as you read. Take your time while reading this short but meaningful book. I would urge you to add it to your religious readings. Dr. Law answers the most important reason to pray....JESUS DID IT.

The Reverend Doctor Phil DeMore
Retired United Methodist minister

While reading this book as part of my devotional every day, I became more and more in awe that God, Creator of the Universe, truly does love us and desires to communicate and build relationship with us. What a source of continuing joy, rebuke, guidance and assurance. This book can speak to 10 year olds and to those who have prayed many years.

Sylvia B. Palmer

Christian Education Learning Center (retired)

Gainesville and Habersham County (GA)

How Prayer Really Works: According to Scripture

Copyright © 2017 FLETCHER LAW. All rights reserved.
Published by RED CLAY BOOKS

ISBN 978-1-387-33830-6

CONTENTS

Psalm 18:6 New King James
Version (NKJV)

"In my distress, I called upon the
Lord, And cried out to my God; He
heard my voice from His temple,
And my cry came before Him,
even to His ears."

The book is dedicated to my
Mother and first worship leader,
Susan Manley Law.
She started to teach me to pray
with "Now I lay me down to
sleep…"

Chapter 1: Do You Need Prayer?

1 Chronicles 16:11

"Seek the Lord and His strength; Seek His face evermore!"

Do you need to pray? That is the easiest argument to win ever. Yes, you need to pray. If you do not think you need to pray, just keep living. If you do not yet feel convinced of the need for prayer, you soon will be. The need to weep, plead, communicate and worship will drive you there. We do things for which we can't forgive ourselves. Things happen to us that we cannot forget or forgive. Life will make you hungry, desperate and pleading to learn how to pray. It is tough enough, so why would you go through your lifetime without prayer? But from what religion, tradition or system will you learn to pray? Few people alive feel they have had the best things life has to offer. So in learning how to pray, you can learn from the Word of the Lord the best way to communicate with Him. You can learn from the Author and Creator of prayer. The old country song said it was foolish to be, "looking for love in all the wrong places." So, why would you look where the answers are not? Learn from the best. Your own trials, unforeseen obstacles and evil influences in your life will challenge you to search out prayer and give you the desire to learn how to pray. Your own heart, soul, and mind cannot help but seek answers, forgiveness, and support that are missing. These all can seem distant and out of reach. Who you are yearning for is not a doctor, policeman, judge, psychiatrist, financial advisor, president, king or queen. What is missing in your search comes only

from a kingdom, a family, a Father –
the very King of kings and Lord of
lords. You may know Him and you
may not have ever heard of Him.
Your soul is in need of
communication with "The Great I
Am" of the Old Testament and "Lord
God Almighty" in the New
Testament. You can have who Jesus
Christ called Abba or Father listen to
your problems. God, The Father
Almighty, Creator of Heaven and

Earth, is the one who will judge the living and the dead one day. He can hear your plea. The Judge, the CEO of all for eternity, can listen to you. Unlike here on earth where people think they are too busy or too important to listen, He will hear your worries with love and compassion. The King is waiting to hear your prayer in His heavenly temple. And what, again, is your reason for not praying?

Psalm 18:6

"In my distress, I called upon the Lord, And cried out to my God; He heard my
voice from His temple, And my cry came before Him, even to His ears."

Do you need prayer? I know I do.

Do you know that you do? As a child, images of death would tie my stomach in knots. These images would come out of nowhere and invade my sense of peace. Young people are taunted with the fear of not fitting in or not belonging to "the in-group." That fear seems to hover over them. Along with the social pressure, they also have to deal with academic pressure. There is immense pressure to be accepted in the best high schools, colleges, or training programs in order to be competitive in the workforce. Adults know getting a job seems easy until you are unemployed. We live in a nation where it is rare for a nuclear family to be intact. All children cannot count on the loving support of both a mother and father. Many grow up to have their own families without ever having had the experience of a healthy and loving family. The onslaught of medical issues, financial difficulties and natural catastrophes can devastate a family. Poverty, tragedy, violence and disease seem to strike not just far away regions and nations, but people we know and love. Often we cannot get over the bad things that have happened to us or the bad things we have done to others. We struggle to live with our actions. We try to live with the consequences of unforgiven sin. People, even loved ones, do strike out to purposely hurt us at times. Your heart, mind, and soul are distraught. But take heart, your appeal can be heard in the highest court!

John 5:14

"Now this is the confidence that we have in Him, that if we ask anything according to His will, He hears us."

Chapter 2: Can You Pray?

Psalm 65:4

"Blessed is the man You choose,
And cause to approach You,
That he may dwell in Your courts.
We shall be satisfied with the
goodness of Your house,
Of Your holy temple."

One day Jesus was "set up" with

a question by some young lawyers.

He had just been in an verbal

sparring session with the religious

legal team, the Pharisees. Next, He

was being confronted by the other religious party of "experts" in Scripture and Jewish law, the Sadducees.

Matthew 22: 15

"The same day the Sadducees, who say there is no resurrection, came to Him and asked ...".

The Pharisees and Sadducees were trying to informally grill Jesus while showing no respect for Him or His answers. They thought Jesus was only a simple carpenter from

Nazareth who was riding a brief wave of popularity in the eyes of the common people of Jerusalem. In this informal press conference the young power-brokers were pressing Jesus with what seemed liked innocent questions about the law of their mutual faith. They asked Jesus a trumped up question about an almost improbable situation. These two groups were hiding their true motives of this informal interrogation. They were planning to trip him up and make him seem foolish about His knowledge of God's Word to the crowd of people watching. Today that is what is called 'gotcha questioning.' This type of questioning seems harmless at first. It is often an attempt to get the subject of the interview to bite on a simple question and say something outrageous and self-destructive. Present day reporters use this type of questioning to trick well known people. Reporters will passively try to embarrass political figures, celebrities or sports figures with seemingly simple questions. The one who asks the question wins as the other one is disgraced by their unreasonable remarks. The questioner walks away and appears to be wiser because he has proven his superior ideas in this informal court. A certain Sadducee asked Jesus this loaded question. Referring to the Old Testament and the Law of Moses, the Sadducee asked about the successive death of seven brothers. The first brother was married and died as later did the second, third, fourth, fifth, sixth and finally the seventh brother. This happened in sequential order. According to the Sadducees' presentation of the Scripture concerning the law of Moses, a brother was commanded to marry his deceased brother's widow. All seven brothers eventually died in first through seventh order and each of the next six brothers did their religious duty by marrying the now seven-time widowed woman. Then the interviewer stated that the woman died. A "gotcha question" was now asked about the woman's marital status in the resurrection. The "gotcha question" the Sadducee's proposed was asked in the book of Matthew.

Matthew 22:28

"Therefore, in the resurrection, whose wife of the seven will she be? For they all had her."

Remember Matthew 22:23? That verse states that the Sadducees did not even believe in the resurrection, much less eternal life or Heaven as we know it from New Testament teaching. The Pharisees, who did believe in the resurrection, were the other Jewish party of power who were professionals in law and religion. They were often called scribes. Both of these groups of "wise scribes" were now ready to hear Jesus' answer and witness Him making a fool of Himself. The Sadducee then stepped back, believing Jesus had been supplied with enough rope to hang Himself because of the brilliant questioning and reasoning. Jesus was supposed to stumble and fall in public from the power of the great wisdom and wit from this self-righteous man. They faked interest in Jesus' answer to an unlikely situation. Whose wife would she be in the resurrection? So this is the question this certain Sadducee presented to Him? This is how he wasted his time in the presence of Jesus Christ, the Messiah?

(No comments were made about any brothers having considered trying to flee from this woman with improbable, yet horrible marital fortunes!)

The Sadducees were buried in religious traditions of the past that taught against a reality of an afterlife, as Christians view it today with promise and hope. The Pharisees were optimistic in searching for a new reason to hope in their progressive view of eternal life. They had been especially put out with

Jesus, as He often publically challenged them on their self-righteousness and self importance. They all gathered around Jesus - I think, with a sense of amusement. They were waiting for the country bumpkin to self-implode. Surely, they reasoned, they would be the ones to interpret Scripture and correctly reason out the end of human life. If anyone had the answers about Scripture, it was them. It certainly would not be this traveling commoner and itinerant preacher. They were wrong. Like many of us – they did not know who they were talking to when talking to God's Son and Savior of the world. Now Jesus gave them His answer. First, He answered their Torah (Jewish Scripture) trivia question in Matthew.

Matthew 22:29-30

"[29] Jesus answered and said to them, "You are mistaken, not knowing the Scriptures nor the power of God. [30] For in the resurrection they neither marry nor are given in marriage, but are like angels of God in heaven."

Next, Jesus answered the real problem that was under the surface between the Pharisees and the Sadducees in Matthew 22:31-32.

RESURRECTION and ETERNAL LIFE!

Matthew 22:31-32

"31 But concerning the resurrection of the dead, have you not read what was spoken to you by God, saying, 32 'I am the God of Abraham, the God of Isaac, and the God of Jacob'? God is not the God of the dead, but of the living."

And what did the crowd think after hearing the answers of Jesus?

Matthew 22:33

"And when the multitudes heard this, they were astonished at His teaching."

Jesus still respected His opponents and talked with them like the earthly men they were. He held nothing back. Some Bible teachers have talked about how Christ hated the Pharisees and Sadducees. Wrong! This is incorrect as Jesus loved them very much. He devoted much time in conversation with them as He intended to minister to all, even the arrogant. Their hypocrisy is not like your enemies' hypocrisy. No, it is like your own hypocrisy and it is like mine. God can work with your hypocrisy when no one else will. Is there anyone so arrogant that you cannot talk to them? You can talk, but you know they will not hear. The Lord knows people like that, us. Jesus Christ, God in the flesh, knows someone like that, you and me. He still died on the cross so you could escape sin, death, and have peace with God. Don't give up on yourself because of your own Pharisee tendencies. Pray for patience. Who has it? The Lord gives patience when we ask for it. Patience is one of the fruits of the Spirit listed in the Bible. Prayer then is our communication with the Almighty.

This communication also includes us

HEARING!!!

Jesus and the Pharisees had different opinions about God. The Pharisees and Sadducees could tell you about God. Jesus Christ knew Him as Abba, Father and Daddy! Today the word Pharisee is given to religious conservatives anytime some group has a dispute with anyone. The Sadducees were only trying to one-up their religious and political rivals - the progressive Pharisees. Jesus turned the inane and frivolous discussion towards substance, not 'religious noise'. He addressed the resurrection of the dead, faith in God, and the eternal life that the Sadducees talked about - but did not have. The real question the men held in their hearts about eternal life and feared to ask was answered in the next verses.

Matthew 22:31-32

"*31* But concerning the resurrection of the dead, have you not read what was spoken to you by God, saying, *32* 'I am the God of Abraham, the God of Isaac, and the

God of Jacob'? God is not the God
of the dead, but of the living."

Later, after the Sadducee's attempt to embarrass Jesus failed, a young Pharisee thought he would win the day with his follow up question. This learned man of reputation felt he was in charge of his life and felt secure in taking Jesus down verbally. He thought he could 'help' Jesus and teach the country boy from Nazareth a thing or two about the law. Then the Pharisee lawyer asked Jesus his question in the book of Matthew.

Matthew 22:36

"Teacher, which is the great commandment in the law?"

Jesus answered and silenced that particular young lawyer by getting to the point.

Matthew 22:37-38

" [37] *Jesus said to him, "You shall love the Lord your God with all your heart, with all your soul, and with all your mind.'* [38] *This is the first and great commandment. "*

Then Jesus took the answer further in verses 39-40.

Matthew 22:39-40

"[39] And the second is like it: 'You shall love your neighbor as yourself.'
[40] *On these two commandments hang all the Law and the Prophets. "*

The One who will judge the souls of the living and dead one day gave the young lawyer the complete verdict. The important things in our lives are always attached to our relationship with Christ. If you want to ask the Lord the "hard question", be prepared to listen as He answers. It has been said – if you call out the bull, you may get the horns. We ask. He answers. The answers might be hard to take if you refuse truth. If you listen, they can be healing. His answers are life changing. We must learn to listen. The answer Jesus Christ gave was not about commandments or following laws. His answer was centered on love. His love for us was demonstrated by coming to earth as a man, teaching, and paying our debt for sin to His Father so we could be made whole. He obeyed His Father to be sacrificed on the cross to pay our sin debt. Now sin no longer separates humans from their Creator Father. This is the love Jesus has for us called GRACE.

The conversation continued with Jesus Christ, the young lawyer and the rest of the Pharisees in Matthew 22.

Matthew 22: 41-45

"[41] While the Pharisees were gathered together, Jesus asked them, [42] saying, "What do you think about the Christ? Whose Son is He?"

"They said to Him, "The Son of David."

43 He said to them, "How then does David in the Spirit call Him 'Lord,' saying:

44 'The LORD said to my Lord, "Sit at My right hand, Till I make Your enemies Your footstool"'?

45 If David then calls Him 'Lord,' how is He his Son?" **46** And no one was able to answer Him a word, nor from that day on did anyone dare question Him anymore."

Jesus Christ never had an identity crisis. We have a crisis when we do not know who He is or what He has done and will do for us. In the Kingdom, we turn to our head, Jesus Christ. This intimate Kingdom is also called a Body – The Body of Christ. To be a citizen of this kingdom, to be included in the family of God, and to be a part of the body of Christ, you need to ask. You need to talk and pray to the Father. To be in a relationship with your King and

Father, you ask and listen. You are afforded that relationship through His Son, Jesus Christ, who cleanses us of our sins when we ask for forgiveness.

He died to pay your sin penalty to the Father, so you may be declared sinless before God and join this heavenly family. We now belong in the kingdom because He declares us sinless, blameless, and holy – after we ask for and receive forgiveness and fellowship.

How do you know someone? You talk to them. You hear them. How do you begin? Speak to them and be prepared to listen.

Speak and listen from your heart, soul and mind.

What if you enter into the conversation with the most Holy with feelings of emptiness? The King has insured plans for this important meeting.

Romans 8:26-27

" [26] *Likewise the Spirit also helps in our weaknesses. For we do not know what we should pray for as we ought, but the Spirit Himself makes*
intercession for us with groanings which cannot be uttered.

²⁷ Now He who searches the hearts knows what the mind of the Spirit is, because He makes intercession for the saints according to the will of God. "

Do you need to talk to someone about your troubles? Do you need to hear from the one with whom you speak or plead your case? Do you understand you can call out to The King of Glory, Father and Abba?

Do you understand that this is a sacred talk with eternal consequences?

This prayer conversation is an act of beautiful worship whether this conversation is in a church, a school, a home, a hospital, a bar or a drug house.

How Do I Know He Answers Prayer?

For myself and others who know Him, we can testify to our answered prayers. These answers are often given in power and sometimes in silence. When we are talking to the King, we need to realize that our prayers probably will not be answered the way we wish they were. A king is fully in charge and does things his way. Our King is fully in charge and will do what is best for you when you are in His will and in His perfect time. The Bible tells of the Lord hearing the cries of the children of Israel in Egypt. They had been in bondage to the Egyptians for over 400 years, until Moses was sent by the Lord to rescue them. Scripture tells how the sick are made whole and captives are freed after prayer. The honest doubter may ask, "How does the mechanism of prayer work? If there is a God, does He really hear me?"

To add to worries about prayer, some Bible teachers have taught that prayer only changes you, not the situation you are in, no matter how desperate it is.

Other Bible teachers have implied that God will do anything you ask. Both extremes contain only partial truth. Yes, you will change when you pray and fellowship with the Most High. Yet, the One who brought the universe into existence made the rain stop for over three years when asked and then started it

back on command.

James 5:17-18

"[17] Elijah was a man with a nature like ours, and he prayed earnestly that it would not rain; and it did not rain on the land for three years and six months. [18] And he prayed again, and the heaven gave rain, and the earth produced its fruit."

All answered prayers are in the

will of God.

Do you remember the Lord's

Prayer in found Matthew 6:10?

Matthew 6:10

"Your kingdom come. Your will be done. On earth as it is in heaven."

The power from heaven then comes to earth. It is true the Lord loves His people and is a loving Father. The King decrees what is best for the kingdom. A father does what is best for his family. He is the king. His answer will be perfect, just, and loving for His family. Are you in His family? Hopefully, you are asking,

"How does prayer actually work?" You say, "I still want the exact mechanics, the conversation, and the interaction with the Holy Spirit. This book led me to believe I would understand how this sacred talk called prayer operates in a manner between humanity and God Almighty! Does He hear me? You are implying the God who is spirit, has ears? You mean He hears and then acts? Is there a real transaction of conversation with an unknowable God?"

Perhaps the greatest frustration for both the Christian and non-Christian is the inability to feel they know how to pray or to feel that prayer actually works. Desperate people really want to know if prayer can help them be whole or is it really just a myth? This is, after all, a jaded, doubting and pessimistic world in which we live. The doubters can have hope. They always have had the answer. There is a place that describes exactly how prayer works.

Where Is Proof of The Mechanics Of Prayer You Promised?

The answer comes from the same place you are told God loves you - in Scripture. Yes, you will be given chapter and verse of how prayer really works. It is found in the last book of the Bible –The Revelation of Jesus Christ or simply, Revelation.

Chapter 3: What Convinces Me Prayer Works?

Psalm 145:18

"The Lord is near to all who call upon Him, To all who call upon Him in truth."

My daily commute to work takes approximately thirty minutes. I teach seventh grade Social Studies. I have joked with friends by telling them that teaching these seventh-grade boys and girls must be some type of

Protestant penance. That early morning drive gives me time to clear my head, pray, and meditate on the task of dealing with this fun, yet highly charged and emotional age group. After listening to the local news and sports radio for weeks, I was looking for a change. I had found an old CD recording of the New Testament. I chose to start with the book of The Revelation of Jesus Christ, or as it is often called, the

Book of Revelation. My intent was to listen closely to the book of Revelation and study the outline. I listened to the chapters over and over. I paid attention to the churches, the seven seals, and the events that will happen before the return of Christ. The Apostle John wrote the book while exiled for his faith by the Roman government on the island of Patmos in the Mediterranean Sea. He was well past the age of 90. He had served as the "beloved disciple" with and during the earthly ministry of Jesus Christ, His Lord. John described what he had seen while caught up in a vision in the very throne room of God and the Lamb, Jesus Christ in chapters five and eight. In these chapters we read how prayers are handled when received by the Lord's angels in Heaven. Those prayers are presented to God. After a time of quiet deliberation, The

Almighty gives His response and verdict. The angels then send the answered prayers back to Earth. We are given an exact and accurate description of how prayer works in Heaven. These prayers were actually seen, and treated by angels as real objects. They were treated with respect and love. I was jolted spiritually when I heard this. This passage filled up my heart, soul, and mind. The Apostle John, who was given access to view the city and the throne room, gave us a portrayal of how our prayers are received by God in Heaven.

As we read in Revelation 4, John heard an angel ask the throngs in Heaven a question. In chapter 5 of Revelation, we see how prayer works.

Revelation 5:2

"Who is worthy to open the scroll and to loose its seals?"

John the Apostle heard how the opened seals would usher in the conclusion of world history. He wept greatly when an angel in his presence asked who could or who was even worthy to break open the sealed scroll from the Lamb.

Revelation 5:4

" ⁴ So I wept much, because no one was found worthy to open and read the scroll, or to look at it."

This sealed scroll has been called the title deed to the world. This was a rhetorical question about who was worthy to bring the Lord's work on earth and time's end to conclusion – to open the seal. The answer was known by all the residents of heaven except for the temporary visitor, John. Except for John, everyone knew the Lamb of God, Jesus, was also the Lion. He was and is The One worthy to rule on all matters and draw the history of the world to an end. The Lion of The Tribe of Judah,

Jesus Christ, who paid for the sins of the world on the cross to save all believers, brought salvation as decreed by His Father. This Lamb of God was slain so our debt of sin could be paid to His Father and we could be declared not guilty. We who believe now are justified before the Father and declared legally sinless. Jesus Christ grants us the privilege to go before His Father in prayer so we can enter into the throne room of the

Lord to present ourselves, and our needs.

Hebrews 4:1

"Let us therefore come boldly to the throne of grace, that we may obtain mercy and find grace to help in time of need."

This includes your prayers. The scripture says we are to come **boldly** to the throne. I believe this means we come to the throne with confidence our loving Father hears us. Perhaps you think your prayers are insignificant. Your prayers are as important as a child's concerns are to a human parent. How much more important are our pleas to the perfect heavenly parent, our Father? He hears us! This same King who will someday end the world paid the ultimate price so you can present your needs to His Father in prayer. The One who was chosen (Jesus Christ) to open the seal is the One who made it so your prayers can be heard in Heaven.

Revelation 5:1-3

" ¹ And I saw in the right hand of Him who sat on the throne a scroll written

inside and on the back, sealed with seven seals. ² Then I saw a strong angel

proclaiming with a loud voice, "Who is worthy to open the scroll and to loose its

seals?" ³ And no one in heaven or on the earth or under the earth was able to open the scroll, or to look at it".

John, the beloved disciple, was just a

human who found himself before

heavenly beings and the King of

kings and Lord of lords. As we read

about this glorious interaction, we find that, quite simply and understandably, John lost it. He lost it emotionally, physically, and spiritually. John wept bitterly.

Revelation 5:4

"So I wept much, because no one was found worthy to open and read the scroll, or to look at it."

I wonder if the angel was amused by John and his mortal behavior before the throne. The throng of worshippers in Glory had always known it was   Jesus Christ, The Messiah. Since the beginning of time, it was the Savior who would rule on all things, especially the conclusion of history and humanity on present earth. This had been decided by the Father from the beginning of time. Then one of the 24 elders before the throne of God set the human straight.

Revelation 5:5

"But one of the elders said to me, "Do not weep. Behold, the Lion of the tribe of Judah, the Root of

David, has prevailed to open the scroll and to loose its seven seals."

Next, a mystical appearance happened and Jesus Christ appeared in the form of a Lamb. How can I explain His appearance? All I can say is we will just have to be there one day and see Him.

Revelation 5:6-7

" [6] And I looked, and behold, in the midst of the throne and of the four living creatures, and in the midst of the elders, stood a Lamb as though it had been slain, having seven horns and seven eyes, which are the seven Spirits of God sent out

into all the earth. ⁷ Then He came and took the scroll out of the right hand of Him who sat on the throne."

This Lamb who now acted as a Lion displayed his battle scars from His death on the cross. This was His display again of His victory on the cross over sin, Satan, hell, and the grave. Yet, we mortals will still not go before the One who desires love, friendship, conversation, and worship with us. We hesitate to bring to Him our life's needs and worries. By pride, self-pity, or the experience of false teachings, we deny ourselves access to our royal brother and lover of humanity.

A Problem, Prayers, and Celebration

This celebration was overwhelming to John. This incomparable celebration and ceremony seems to be the norm in Heaven. First comes problems, second comes presentations of prayers, and third comes celebrations as the Champion of Heaven decrees

victory.

Revelation 5:8-14

"[8] Now when He had taken the scroll, the four living creatures and the twenty-four elders fell down before the Lamb, each having a harp, and golden bowls full of incense, which are the prayers of the saints. [9] And they sang a new song, saying:

"You are worthy to take the scroll,

And to open its seals; For You were slain,

And have redeemed us to God by Your blood

Out of every tribe and tongue and people and nation,

^{10} *And have made us kings and priests to our God;*

And we shall reign on the earth."

^{11} *Then I looked, and I heard the voice of many angels around the throne, the living creatures, and the elders; and the number of them was ten thousand times ten thousand, and thousands of thousands,* ^{12} *saying with a loud voice: "Worthy is the Lamb who was slain To receive power and riches and wisdom,*

And strength and honor and glory and blessing!"

^{13} *And every creature which is in heaven and on the earth and under the earth and such as are in the sea, and all that are in them, I heard saying:*

"Blessing and honor and glory and power Be to Him who sits on the throne,

And to the Lamb, forever and ever!"

14 Then the four living creatures said, "Amen!" And the twenty-four elders fell down and worshiped Him who lives forever and ever."

Chapter 4: How Does Prayer Work In Scripture?

Revelation 8:4

"And the smoke of the incense, with the prayers of the saints, ascended before God from the angel's hand."

You have read the promise on the cover of this book of how prayer physically and supernaturally happens in the throne room of God according to Holy Scripture.

" ¹ When He opened the seventh seal, there was silence in heaven for about half an hour. ² And I saw the seven angels who stand before God, and to them were given seven trumpets. ³ Then another angel, having a golden censer, came and stood at the altar. He was given much incense, that he should offer it with the prayers of all the saints upon the golden altar which was before the throne. ⁴ And the smoke of the incense, with the prayers of the saints, ascended before God from the angel's hand. ⁵ Then the angel took the censer, filled it with fire from the altar, and threw it to the earth. And there were noises, thunderings, lightnings, and an earthquake."

Let's Break Down This Heavenly Prayer Transaction

First-John reports there is holy silence, reverence, and awe about what is to take place before the throne of God as recorded.

Revelation 8:1

" When He opened the seventh seal, there was silence in heaven for about half an hour."

Second-Angels, along with John, stand before God in Heaven to serve at His command.

John recorded this:

Revelation 8:2.

" And I saw the seven angels who stand before God, and to them were given seven trumpets."

Third- Prayers are ignited on the

golden altar before the throne of God.

Revelation 8:3

"Then another angel, having a golden censer, came and stood at the altar. He was given much incense, that he should offer it with the prayers of all the saints upon the golden altar which was before the throne."

Did you get that? Prayers are mixed and burned with incense in a golden censer by angels on a golden altar before the throne of God. Yes, that is right. Your prayers are burned!

Fourth- The smoke of the incense and prayers of the saints (God's people) rise up to God as an aroma.

Revelation 8:4

"And the smoke of the incense, with the prayers of the saints, ascended before God from the angel's hand."

Yes, that is right. God receives your prayers through His nostrils! That is personal.

Fifth- God takes in the aroma of your prayers and contemplates the prayers silently. He alone decides the answer of the prayers.

Sixth- God answers and His angel delivers the answer to prayers to our world.

Revelation 5:5

"Then the angel took the censer, filled it with fire from the altar, and threw it to the earth. And there were noises, thunderings, lightnings, and an earthquake."

The answers to prayer are returned to earth from the throne of God. The angel of God takes the embers of the burnt and charred prayers. Then the angel fills the golden censer from the golden altar and throws the contents of the censor (the burnt embers of spent prayers) to earth. So, the answer to your prayers comes from Heaven to Earth! Yes, just like it says in the Model or Lord's Prayer in Matthew 6:10 " *...Your will be done On earth as it is in heaven.*"

Seventh- The prayers are answered in the way the King decrees them to be answered. The strong angel hurls the answered prayers back to earth, according to Revelation. Now we can conclude that we receive the answers in His time. In this holy, incredible, supernatural event of prayers being received and answered by God, our modern sensibilities must be shocked. Prayers are not positive thoughts or vibes mentally transmitted by good intentions. Prayers, according to Revelation 8:1-5, are tangible elements in the heavenly kingdom before the throne of God. Get this - God values your prayers. The strong angel mixes your prayers in a golden bowl and they are burned on a golden censer on the heavenly altar before God Almighty's throne! God smells the aroma of our prayers as they rise in His throne room. The strong angel then takes the censer after filling it with fire, hurls the contents and the prayers flow back to earth. In this case, the prayers deal with events of the end of history of this present age.

Are all the prayers presented before The Lord of value? It reads in Revelation that the prayers of the saints are presented. Those prayers are from His people. These prayers are from people for whom His Son Jesus Christ died. The prayers are valuable because He loves His children. The ancient Hebrews tried to obey strict modes of conduct and worship. They fell short and often were unfaithful by following false gods and evil desires. These ancient people of God were wracked with guilt as they could not maintain the effort to worship perfectly with their actions, prayers, and live animal sacrifices. They were never in full communion with the Lord, as we all can be after the time of Christ on earth. The Lord worked through revelations at specific times in the Old Testament. At that time, only a selected few of the Lord's faithful were connected and empowered with the Holy Spirit. The once and for all payment of sin by Jesus Christ had not yet been paid for His people and all people who would believe the gospel of Christ. Animal sacrifices in Old Testament temple worship were just a foreshadowing of the permanent forgiveness to come through Jesus Christ in the New Testament. The Holy Spirit was sent to believers only after the sacrifice of

Jesus Christ on the cross. His resurrection and ascension back to Heaven and the gift of the Holy Spirit was given to all believers in the Holy Spirit at Pentecost. The Holy Spirit continues to draw people to Christ today! The Holy Spirit mediates our prayers, along with Christ Jesus. Prayer and direct access to the Lord is available to all believers now. Through the Holy Spirit believers can draw near to the throne room of God.

Finally, in the New Testament the true essential way to worship was shared by the Jewish Jesus of Nazareth to an outcast woman of another ethnic and religious group. Christ Jesus told the Samaritan woman in John 4 that in the future we would worship and commune through SPIRIT and TRUTH. God is Spirit and He deals only in truth. In truth is the only way we can worship Him and communicate with Him through prayer. That is how we need to approach Him. We present the truth in our confession of sins, problems and our thanksgiving. Truth is heard in our spirit by the Holy Father, The Lord God. The Lord can then do His work for us when we confess to Him in truth. What we receive from the Lord is truth.

Chapter 5: How Do I Pray?

Luke 11:1

"...Lord, teach us to pray, as John also taught his disciples."

"How do I pray?" This is the question that quite simply panics and stops many people from praying. People have great reservations about the greatest privilege and right the Lord gives to His children. Some people look for models from prayer books or from traditions of the ancient church. That could be a good start. By themselves, many people believe they are completely unequipped and that they must have the endorsement and format of a formally trained clergy to learn to pray.

Other people and some church traditions scoff and totally refuse to endorse any prewritten prayer or pattern from church history. Those against using a model of a formatted pattern of prayer often view that type of prayer as inauthentic, powerless and devoid of the Holy Spirit's influence.

I learned a hard life lesson when my vocation and future were once in jeopardy. The lesson I learned was to share with Him what made me hurt and fear in all areas of my life. He needed me to love and worship Him in the manner He wanted me to and that is established in His Word, the Holy Bible.

Matthew 22:37

"Jesus said to him, "You shall love the Lord your God with all your heart, with all your soul, and with all your mind."

I was upset and thought I was doing God's will. I was mad but not expressing it.

You can go to the Lord with your hurts. You can even be mad at Him. Why? He commands for us to do this.

Psalm 55:22

"Cast your burden on the Lord, And He shall sustain you;
He shall never permit the righteous to be moved."

1 Peter 5:6-7

"Therefore humble yourselves under the mighty hand of God, that He may exalt you in due time, [7] casting all your care upon Him, for He cares for you."

A dilemma is presented here. We all have hurts and still have needs. The Devil, others, and we ourselves cause us to feel unworthy to pray.

Again, here comes the lock-down at our attempts to pray. What can pull us out of the unworthy feelings of self-accusation? It is this simple. Look to Jesus. He gives you the right to pray in SPIRIT AND TRUTH. So, whom can we look to as a model for prayer?

How about God's only Son, Jesus Christ? The King made your way to pray. This prayer He taught is universally known as the Lord's

Prayer. Many refer to it as the Model Prayer. Jesus Christ's very own disciples had seen Him raise the dead, walk on water, heal the sick and lame, give sight to the blind and heal a deaf mute. What did the Christ's disciples ask Jesus to teach them?

Luke 11: 1

"Lord, teach us to pray, …"

Why? They saw God's only Son live a victorious and meaningful life devoted to prayer. So why did they ask Jesus to teach them how to pray? These men saw the results of prayer in His life.

Their Rabbi, Jesus, had peace, fellowship with the Father, and power in life. When asked, Jesus Christ taught His disciples the Lord's Prayer or the Model Prayer. He taught them the format of prayer that is found in Matthew 6:9-13.

The Lord's Prayer or Model Prayer

Matthew 6:9-13

"9 In this manner, therefore, pray:

Our Father in heaven,

Hallowed be Your name.

10 Your kingdom come.

Your will be done

On earth as it is in heaven.

11 Give us this day our daily bread.

12 And forgive us our debts,

As we forgive our debtors.

13 And do not lead us into temptation,

But deliver us from the evil one.

For Yours is the kingdom and the power and the glory forever. Amen.

Matthew 6:9
"In this manner, therefore, pray: ..."

Address the One you speak to intimately as "our Father". In this case, it is The Lord Almighty. He has the most impressive address ever to send a letter or any communication, Heaven.

"Our Father in heaven,"

His name is special. His name is the name of the creator of life and our Lord. His name brings salvation, healing and help.

"Hallowed be Your name."

You are acknowledging to The King that you understand His role and yours in the kingdom. You understand the best possible situation will come from being in His will.

"¹⁰ Your kingdom come. Your will be done"

You are acknowledging His will shall be done and that you are in agreement with Him. Then, you are acknowledging Him and to yourself that you know His jurisdiction- Earth and Heaven.

"On earth as it is in heaven."

You are acknowledging that His power, and His solution are sent from Heaven to Earth as stated in Revelation. Every second of your life depends on His providing for you.

"11 Give us this day our daily bread."

You humbly ask for forgiveness.

"12 And forgive us our debts, "As we forgive our debtors."

You are acknowledging your need for His mercy and grace. When you receive MERCY and GRACE, you are then required to extend mercy and grace to others. You need to change and grow spiritually. These are His conditions for growth.

"13 And do not lead us into temptation,"

You are asking to be kept from sinning and to be made aware of any actions that can yield bad consequences and to flee from them!

"But deliver us from the evil one."

You are asking for His protection from the evil one and forces of evil.

"For Yours is the kingdom and the power and the glory forever."

You are pledging to Him and reminding yourself that as a Christian you are part of an eternal kingdom. You believe this.

"Amen."

People will continually feel inadequate when talking to God.

Let's face it, you and I are inadequate to talk to God because we are mere humans. Why would the King of all creation want to, decide to, and even demand to talk with us? Why? Our King knows and loves us. We can do nothing for His benefit. Why does He care for us? For no good reason, other than because of His wondrous unmerited favor and love called GRACE!!! Our King dwelled with us once on earth and now dwells in

Heaven. He embodies all that is good

and is full of two of the most

beautiful words – grace and truth.

John 1:14

"And the Word became flesh and dwelt among us, and we beheld His glory, the glory as of the only begotten of the Father, full of grace and truth."

Again, one common weakness of

the human race is their great

hesitancy to go to the Lord in prayer.

Do you still feel so unworthy that you can't go to the Him in prayer? In John 4, we are told how a social outcast came to the Lord in prayer. Jesus approached this woman who was of another ethnic and religious group. He sat with her and talked with her. This woman was known as an outcast because of her country, religion, gender, and notorious reputation for her immoral behavior. Our Savior's own people, the Jews, derisively called this woman's people, the Samaritans, half-breeds – the ultimate personal insult. It was strongly implied by society that she never could or would be accepted. The woman's reputation for sexual immorality in her village made her an outcast from her people and her community. In John 7, our Savior sits at the community well in the middle of town at midday with this Samaritan woman and does what? He talks with her about salvation and how to worship. Jesus Christ knew her problems and talked with her, despite society's opinion of her public sin. Read and hear this awesome play by play account from the lips of Jesus who opened prayer to all people.

John 4: 5-26

" ⁵ So He came to a city of Samaria which is called Sychar, near the plot of ground that Jacob gave to his son Joseph.

⁶ Now Jacob's well was there. Jesus therefore, being wearied from His journey, sat thus by the well. It was about the sixth hour.

⁷ A woman of Samaria came to draw water. Jesus said to her, "Give Me a drink."

⁸ For His disciples had gone away into the city to buy food.

⁹ Then the woman of Samaria said to Him, "How is it that You, being a Jew, ask a drink from me, a Samaritan woman?" For Jews have no dealings with Samaritans.
¹⁰ Jesus answered and said to her, "If you knew the gift of God, and who it is who says to you, 'Give Me a drink,' you would have asked Him, and He would have given you living water."

¹¹ The woman said to Him, "Sir, You have nothing to draw with, and the well is deep. Where then do You get that living water?

¹² Are You greater than our father Jacob, who gave us the well, and drank from it himself, as well as his sons and his livestock?"

¹³ Jesus answered and said to her, "Whoever drinks of this water will thirst again,

¹⁴ but whoever drinks of the water that I shall give him will never thirst. But the water that I shall give him will become in him a fountain of water springing up into everlasting life."

¹⁵ The woman said to Him, "Sir, give me this water, that I may not thirst, nor come here to draw."

¹⁶ Jesus said to her, "Go, call your husband, and come here."

¹⁷ The woman answered and said, "I have no husband." Jesus said to her, "You have well said, 'I have no husband,'

¹⁸ for you have had five husbands, and the one whom you now have is not your husband; in that you spoke truly."

¹⁹ The woman said to Him, "Sir, I perceive that You are a prophet.

²⁰ Our fathers worshiped on this mountain, and you Jews say that in Jerusalem is the place where one ought to worship."

²¹ Jesus said to her, "Woman, believe Me, the hour is coming when you will neither on this mountain,

nor in Jerusalem, worship the Father.

22 You worship what you do not know; we know what we worship, for salvation is of the Jews.

23 But the hour is coming, and now is, when the true worshipers will worship the Father in spirit and truth; for the Father is seeking such to worship Him.
24 God is Spirit, and those who worship Him must worship in spirit and truth."

25 The woman said to Him, "I know that Messiah is coming" (who is called Christ). "When He comes, He will tell us all things."

26 Jesus said to her, "I who speak to you am He." "

Can you pray? Yes. Why? Jesus gives you the right. What are your qualifications to approach God? From the Holy Scriptures, we are instructed to be a worshipper. Are you a worshipper?

John 4:23

"But the hour is coming, and now is, when the true worshipers will worship the Father in spirit and truth; for the Father is seeking such to worship Him."

We are to pray. First, it is with a <u>worship</u>ful attitude. Secondly, it is with the understanding that this is a spiritual act as The Holy Spirit transmits this talk. Thirdly, it is knowing that truth is the fuel of prayer. You talk TRUTH to the Lord. No yea-but excuses are allowed. It is now time for truth and confession of sins and, then, requests.

Chapter 6:
What Do I Pray?

1 John 5:14

"Now this is the confidence that we have in Him, that if we ask anything according to His will, He hears us."

A purpose of this book is to urge people to pray. My prayer is that this book has encouraged you to engage in a life of prayer. What should you pray for? Pray about everything involving your life.

There are various lists of types of prayer listed in the Bible. Some books list four, six, eight or twelve types of prayer. Jesus prayed fervently in private and in front of His disciples. In prayer, Christ Jesus celebrated, lamented, and asked for things from His Father. Just like you need to do, Jesus spoke to His Father from His heart. He gave a model prayer when asked by His disciples to teach them how to pray. So, pray.

What topics were off-limits to take to the Lord in prayer? Here is the list. NOTHING! Not one thing. Does this mean you will always pray perfectly? No.

What this does mean is that you will grow in prayer and your prayer life will improve as you pray. Prayer is not for those on the sidelines of faith or life. You may have heard of the old saying, "Prayer changes things." That is true. Interestingly, one of the main things prayer will change is you. Prayer can shape your attitude. Make no mistake about it. The Lord God, King of all, can change your situation. The great prophet of the Old Testament, Elijah, was remembered for his prayer when he asked God to change a situation. In the New Testament the Apostle James recalls the great Elijah and his earnest prayer.

James 5:16

" Elijah was a man with a nature like ours, and he prayed earnestly that it would not rain; and it did not rain on the land for three years and six months. 15 And he prayed again, and the heaven gave rain, and the earth produced its fruit."

You are communicating with the source of ultimate wisdom and knowledge when you pray. In this holy and sacred conversation, you will know more of the previously unknown God. You have an advocate in Jesus. You are never praying alone.

1 John 2:1

"My little children, these things I write to you, so that you may not sin. And if anyone sins, we have an Advocate with the Father, Jesus Christ the righteous."

And Jesus Christ said -

John 14:15-18

" [15] "If you love Me, keep My commandments. [16] And I will pray the Father, and He will give you another Helper, that He may abide with you forever— [17] the Spirit of

truth, whom the world cannot receive, because it neither sees Him nor knows Him; but you know Him, for He dwells with you and will be in you. ¹⁸ I will not leave you orphans; I will come to you."

As it has been said earlier, nothing is off limits to ask. Additionally, you have the Son and Holy Spirit assisting you in prayer to the Father. (Prayer is all about participation - speaking and hearing – being in the moment and being all in.) Jesus Christ gave His all on the cross. In prayer, you give Him the all of your heart, soul, and mind. More than once you will misspeak in prayer; however, you will also grow in prayer. That is expected. You will grow in faith and will be born again as a baby. The Lord will raise you in faith and grace. Our heavenly Father will mature us as we continue our relationship with Him. This is why we have a relationship with the fullness of God as the Father, as the Son, and as the Holy Spirit.

Descriptions of Types of Prayer With Scripture Examples

Prayers of Faith:

Believers ask or make a request to the Lord. These types of prayer are especially for illness and extreme situations. (James 5:15, Hebrews 11:1, Mark 9:23-24)

Prayers of Agreement:

People agree and submit to go to the Lord (petition) together seeking the direction of the Lord to solve their problem. (Matthew 18:19, Acts 1:14, Acts 2:42)

Prayers of Request (or Supplication):

We are to take our requests to God. Our unique problems are presented. We humbly bow on our knees to petition and to beg for help by crying out to our loving Father. (Philippians 4:6, Ephesians 6:18)

Prayers of Thanksgiving:

We give praise and thanks for what He has done already and will continue to do in our life. (Philippians 4:5, Acts 13:2-3).

Prayers of Consecration:

Consecration prayers set apart a marriage, a new job, a new school year for the Lord. We ask The Lord to bless a new endeavor as we are in covenant or a relationship with Him.

(Matthew 26:39).

In John 17, Jesus intercedes on behalf of His followers to the Lord. We pray for other (1Timothy 2:1)

The Prayer of Imprecation:

Imprecatory prayers ask for the vengeance of God to be shown and His holy name to triumph or evil. We ask God to intercede and stop evil actions. We ask the Lord to stop the wicked and their plans as stated in Psalms. (Psalm 7, 55 ,69). This is not an evil request but promotes the righteousness of God. Jesus says to pray for our enemies also. Many feel the New Testament commands us not to pray against other humans. (Matthew 5:44-48)

Praying in The Spirit:

Praying in the Spirit is when we know our mind is not right about things. When we are at our end physically, mentally and spiritually, we must especially pray. When we are at our weakest, this prayer will probably be our best prayer. How can that be said? The Spirit Himself prays for us. (1 Corinthians 14:14-15, Romans 8:26-27)

Chapter 7: Does God Hear You?

Psalm 18:6

"In my distress I called upon the Lord, And cried out to my God;
He heard my voice from His temple, And my cry came before Him, even to His ears."

In my young adult life, I decided to drop out of college. Later, I made the wise decision to finish and to graduate. I returned this time along my wife and infant son. As a returning college student, I had to meet with the Dean for readmission. Understandably, I was concerned about the updated graduation requirements since my departure from school. In my anxiety, I blurted out my worries and anxieties in rapid fashion. The Dean shocked me with his response. "Slow down, I want to listen to you. If you slow down, I will listen to you." He then said quite strongly, "Slow down, I will hear you." For a moment, his words stunned me.

For most of my life, I have had a problem with my speech. Fast, rapid talking was a pattern of my speech, as it is for many others. Trying to get more words in a conversation does not mean that anyone will listen to you. I have since learned that fast-talking speech patterns stem from anxiety. These feelings of anxiety could be based on past experiences or from the assumption that the person you are talking to will not or does not want to hear what you are saying.

Do you fear no one will hear you? Are you alone or feel alone? Do you think there is no way anyone could help? Do you wonder if there is anyone out there who can understand your unique problems? If this is what you are thinking, here is the good news.

Hebrews 4:14-15

"Seeing then that we have a great High Priest who has passed through the heavens, Jesus the Son of God, let us hold fast our confession. ^{15} For we do not have a High Priest who cannot sympathize with our weaknesses, but was in all points tempted as we are, yet without sin."

He knows you and does understand your situation because He knew your sins on the cross. Christ Jesus is not just guessing about your sins, hurts and feelings of anguish. He became sin on the cross and knew your sin, shame, and guilt, even before you were born. Having this knowledge, you can no longer say that no one has ever done anything for you, understands you, or truly knows you. Jesus Christ gave His life on the cross so that you could have peace with the Father. By going to the cross, He paid for your sins. Now your sins are forgiven when you present them in spirit and truth through prayer.

Isaiah 43:16

"Thus says the Lord, who makes a way in the sea
And a path through the mighty waters,"

Jesus Christ made a way to have your plea heard and answered by His Father.

He Hears Our Prayers

Psalm 18:6

"In my distress I called upon the Lord, And cried out to my God;
He heard my voice from His temple, And my cry came before Him, even to His ears."

1 John 5:14-15

" ¹⁴Now this is the confidence that we have in Him, that if we ask anything according to His will, He hears us. ¹⁵ And if we know that He hears us, whatever we ask, we know that we have the petitions that we have asked of Him. "

James 4:3

" You ask and do not receive, because you ask amiss, that you may spend it on your pleasures. "

1 Thessalonians 5:17

"Pray without ceasing, "

Isaiah 65:24

"It shall come to pass That before they call, I will answer; And while they are still speaking, I will hear."

John 15:7

"If you abide in Me, and My words abide in you, you will ask what you desire, and it shall be done for you."

Hebrews 11:6

"But without faith it is impossible to please Him, for he who comes to God must believe that He is, and that He is a rewarder of those who diligently seek Him."

Matthew 21:21

" So Jesus answered and said to them, "Assuredly, I say to you, if you have faith and do not doubt, you will not only do what was done to the fig tree, but also if you say to this mountain, 'Be removed and be cast into the sea,' it will be done."

John 5:30

" I can of Myself do nothing. As I hear, I judge; and My judgment is righteous, because I do not seek My own will but the will of the Father who sent Me."

Micah 7:7

"Therefore I will look to the Lord;I will wait for the God of my salvation; My God will hear me."

Psalm 55:22

"Cast your burden on the Lord, And He shall sustain you; He shall never permit the righteous to be moved."

Chapter 8: Why Are You Not Praying?

Acts 6:4

"But we will give ourselves continually to prayer, and to the ministry of the word."'

You have learned from John 4:24 that the Lord hears those who pray with a worshipful attitude in spirit and truth. What do you want to share with Him?

Please read the following list of some of the wonderful, comforting, and life-giving Scriptures. I pray you will follow the Word of God so you will have prayers that have power. You will need your answer to come from God to be authenticated by the truthfulness of His Word. Listed are the following Scriptures for prayers which focus on specific needs, listed with verses on which you can read, pray and meditate. It is my earnest desire that you will grow in spirit and truth through praying to the King of kings and Lord of lords. Be strong in your salvation and have peace with the Lord and yourself.

Salvation - Sickness and disease – Financial problems – Family problems –Physical Safety - Worry and Anxiety

*Scripture for these subjects are listed on the following pages.

Salvation

John 3:16

"For God so loved the world that He gave His only begotten Son, that whoever believes in Him should not perish but have everlasting life."

John 14:6

"Jesus said to him, "I am the way, the truth, and the life. No one comes to the Father except through Me."

Romans 5:8

"But God demonstrates His own love toward us, in that while we were still sinners, Christ died for us."

Romans 8:1

"There is therefore now no condemnation to those who are in Christ Jesus, who do not walk according to the flesh, but according to the Spirit."

Romans 10:9

"That if thou shalt confess with thy mouth the Lord Jesus, and shalt believe in thine heart that God hath raised him from the dead, thou shalt be saved."

Matthew 19:25-26

"*25 When His disciples heard it, they were greatly astonished, saying, "Who then can be saved?"26 But Jesus looked at them and said to them, "With men this is impossible, but with God all things are possible."*

Hebrews 7:25

"*Therefore He is also able to save to the uttermost those who come to God through Him, since He always lives to make intercession for them.*"

Sickness and Disease

Exodus 23:25

"So you shall serve the Lord your God, and He will bless your bread and your water. And I will take sickness away from the midst of you."

Proverbs 4:20-22

"[20] My son, give attention to my words; Incline your ear to my sayings. [21] Do not let them depart from your eyes; Keep them in the midst of your heart; [22] For they are life to those who find them, and health to all their flesh."

Psalm 30: 1-3

"¹I will extol You, O Lord, for You have lifted me up, and have not let my foes rejoice over me. ² O Lord my God, I cried out to You, and You healed me.

³ O Lord, You brought my soul up from the grave;

You have kept me alive, that I should not go down to the pit."

Psalm 107:19-21

"¹⁹ Then they cried out to the Lord in their trouble, And He saved them out of their distresses. ²⁰ He sent His word and healed them, And delivered them from their destructions. ²¹ Oh, that men would give thanks to the Lord for His goodness, And for His wonderful works to the children of men!"

James 5:13-18

"*13 Is anyone among you suffering? Let him pray. Is anyone cheerful? Let him sing psalms. 14 Is anyone among you sick? Let him call for the elders of the church, and let them pray over him, anointing him with oil in the name of the Lord. 15 And the prayer of faith will save the sick, and the Lord will raise him up. And if he has committed sins, he will be forgiven. 16 Confess your trespasses to one another, and pray for one another, that you may be healed. The effective, fervent prayer of a righteous man avails much. 17 Elijah was a man with a nature like ours, and he prayed earnestly that it would not rain; and it did not rain on the land for three years and six months. 18 And he prayed again, and the heaven gave rain, and the earth produced its fruit.*"

Financial Problems

Malachi 3:10

"Bring all the tithes into the storehouse, That there may be food in My house, And try Me now in this," Says the Lord of hosts, "If I will not open for you the windows of heaven And pour out for you such blessing That there will not be room enough to receive it."

Proverbs 3:9-10

" [9] Honor the Lord with your possessions, And with the first fruits of all your increase; [10] So your barns will be filled with plenty, And your vats will overflow with new wine."

Proverbs 3:27

"Do not withhold good from those to whom it is due,
When it is in the power of your hand to do so."

Matthew 6:33

"But seek ye first the kingdom of God, and his righteousness; and all these things shall be added unto you."

Luke 6:38

"Give, and it will be given to you: good measure, pressed down, shaken together, and running over will be put into your bosom. For with the same measure that you use, it will be measured back to you."

Philippians 4:19

"¹⁹And my God shall supply all your need according to his riches in glory by Christ Jesus."

Family Problems

Joshua 24:15

"And if it seems evil to you to serve the Lord, choose for yourselves this day whom you will serve, whether the gods which your fathers served that were on the other side of the River, or the gods of the Amorites, in whose land you dwell. But as for me and my house, we will serve the Lord."

Psalm 103:17

"But the mercy of the Lord is from everlasting to everlasting On those who fear Him, And His righteousness to children's children,"

Proverbs 6:20

"My son, keep your father's command, And do not forsake the law of your mother."

Psalm 103:17

"But the mercy of the Lord is from everlasting to everlasting On those who fear Him, And His righteousness to children's children,"

Proverbs 11:29

"He who troubles his own house will inherit the wind,
And the fool will be servant to the wise of heart."

Luke 12:32

"Do not fear, little flock, for it is your Father's good pleasure to give you the kingdom."

Galatians 4:4-7

" [4] But when the fullness of the time had come, God sent forth His Son, born of a woman, born under the law, [5] to redeem those who were under the law, that we might receive the adoption as sons

.⁶ And because you are sons, God has sent forth the Spirit of His Son into your hearts, crying out, "Abba, Father!"

⁷ Therefore you are no longer a slave but a son, and if a son, then an heir of God through Christ."

Hebrews 13:5

"Let your conduct be without covetousness; be content with such things as you have. For He Himself has said, "I will never leave you nor forsake you."

Physical Safety

Psalm 5:11

"But let all those rejoice who put their trust in You; Let them ever

shout for joy, because You defend them; Let those also who love Your name Be joyful in You."

Psalm 18:30

"As for God, His way is perfect; The word of the Lord is proven;
He is a shield to all who trust in Him."
Psalm 59:1-2

"1 Deliver me from my enemies, O my God; Defend me from those who rise up against me.[2] Deliver me from the workers of iniquity, And save me from bloodthirsty men."

2 Thessalonians 3:3

"But the Lord is faithful, who will establish you and guard you from the evil one."

1 Peter 2:9

"But you are a chosen generation, a royal priesthood, a holy nation, His own special people, that you may proclaim the praises of Him who called you out of darkness into His marvelous light;"

Worry and Anxiety

Psalm 3:5-6

" [5] I lay down and slept; I awoke, for the Lord sustained me.
[6] I will not be afraid of ten thousands of people Who have set themselves against me all around."

Philippians 4:6- 7

" *⁶ Be anxious for nothing, but in everything by prayer and supplication, with thanksgiving, let your requests be made known to God; ⁷ and the peace of God, which surpasses all understanding, will guard your hearts and minds through Christ Jesus.* "

About The Author

Fletcher Law lives in Gainesville, GA and is a preacher, pastor, evangelist, and teacher. He earned his Doctor of Ministry from Beeson Divinity School at Samford University and his Master of Divinity from Candler School of Theology at Emory University. He also earned his Master of Education from the University of North Georgia. He is an alumnus of the University of Mississippi (Ole Miss), having earned his Bachelor of Education.

To contact Fletcher about this book or speaking engagements for your church, Sunday School class, Christian organization, or sports team please contact him at
redclaybooks@gmail.com